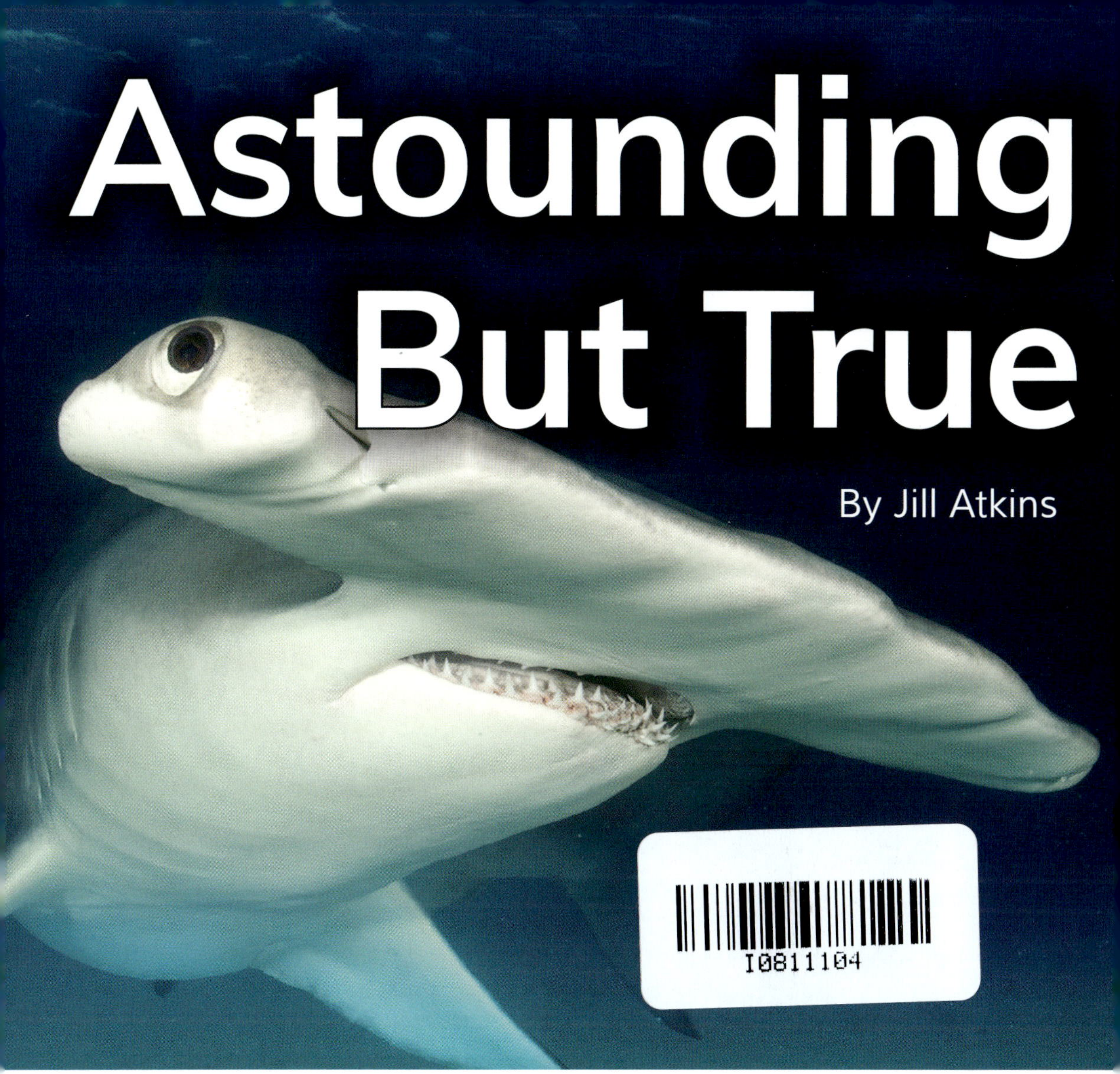

# Astounding But True

By Jill Atkins



Published in 2026 by
**Norwood House Press**
2544 Clinton Street
Buffalo, NY 14224



Printed in the United States of America

Library of Congress Cataloging-in-Publication Data:
Names: Atkins, Jill (Children's author). | Chalik, Chris, illustrator.
Title: Astounding but true / by Jill Atkins. Time for Oscar / written by Jill Atkins, illustrated by Chris Chalik.
Description: Buffalo, NY : Norwood House Press, 2026. | Series: Phonics all-stars: phase 5b
Identifiers: ISBN 9781978578142 (pbk.) | ISBN 9781978578159 (library bound) | ISBN 9781978578166 (ebook)
Subjects: LCSH: Reading–Phonetic method–Juvenile literature. | English language–Phonetics–Juvenile literature. | Curiosities and wonders–Juvenile literature. | Fathers and sons–Juvenile fiction.
Classification: LCC LB1573.3 A796 2026 | DDC 372.465–dc23

CPSIA compliance information: Batch #CW26NHP: For further information contact Norwood House Press at 1-800-237-9932.

When you think about a hippopotamus, you might think of one being in the water.

However, it is an astounding fact that hippos cannot swim! They just do a sluggish gallop on the river bed.

Plus, we think that hippos can sleep under water. They just bob up to take some air – without even needing to wake up!

Hippos can open their mouths so wide, a sports car might fit inside!

Astounding!

A lightning bolt is five times hotter than the sun.

That's astonishing!

Sharks must be the coolest critters in the sea.

So you might not be amazed to hear that sharks can blink. The rest of the fish in the seas and rivers cannot do this.

A shark can get up to 30,000 teeth in its lifetime.

(The teeth drop out, so the fresh ones have room to appear.)

Hamsters' teeth never drop out. They just keep getting longer and longer.

So the hamster must grind its teeth down on hard things like nuts and seeds.

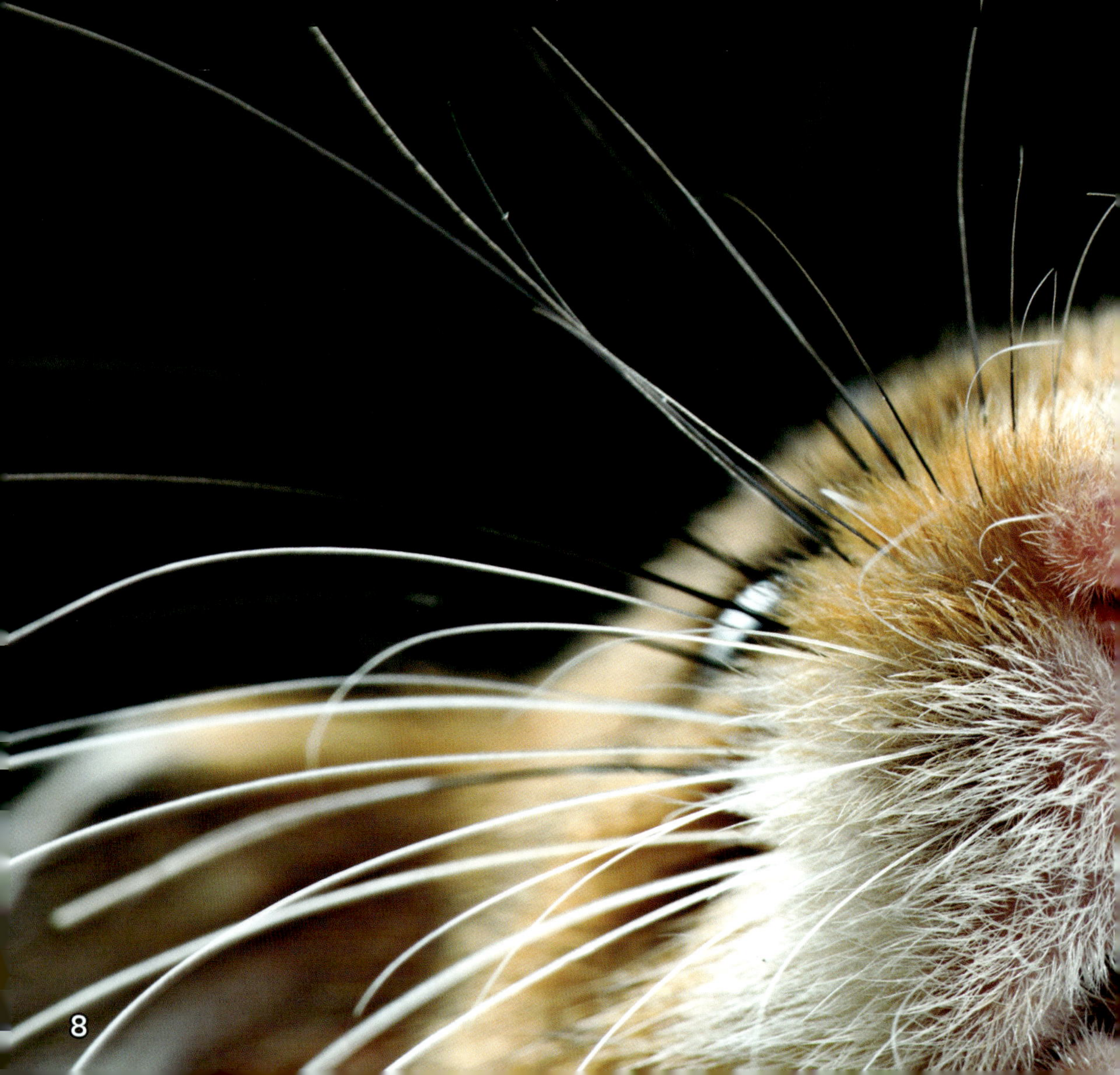

If the teeth get too long, they need to be trimmed – a bit like how we get a haircut.

What a thought!

As we are discussing teeth ...
Do you have snails in the garden? Well, this is a striking fact. Snails have teeth.

You can't see their teeth, even if they smile, but in fact snails have at least a thousand teeth.

They are so little that they are quite like a nail file.

Astounding, but true.

What will you see if you shave a tiger?

Stripes! Tigers have striped fur, but they have striped skin underneath too. The fur and the stripes together make the pattern. That's astounding.

Each tiger has a distinct stripe pattern too. It's a kind of fingerprint!

Flamingos aren't born pink. They turn pink due to the food they eat. (Most of all, it's shrimps that turn them pink.)

As the food goes through the flamingos, it turns them pink!

Let me tell you about the biggest fossilized poo ever found. (You do wish to hear about this, don't you?)

The poo was dug up in Canada. It was almost a foot long and came from a T-Rex.

People found chunks of crushed bone in it, telling us what the T-Rex had for dinner on the day it died!

Can you think of some astounding facts about us?

I'll start. Identical twins are **never** identical – even if they look the same. Each twin will have distinct fingerprints.

Now it's time for you to think of some mind-boggling astounding facts.

# Time for Oscar

Written by Jill Atkins

Illustrated by Chris Chalik

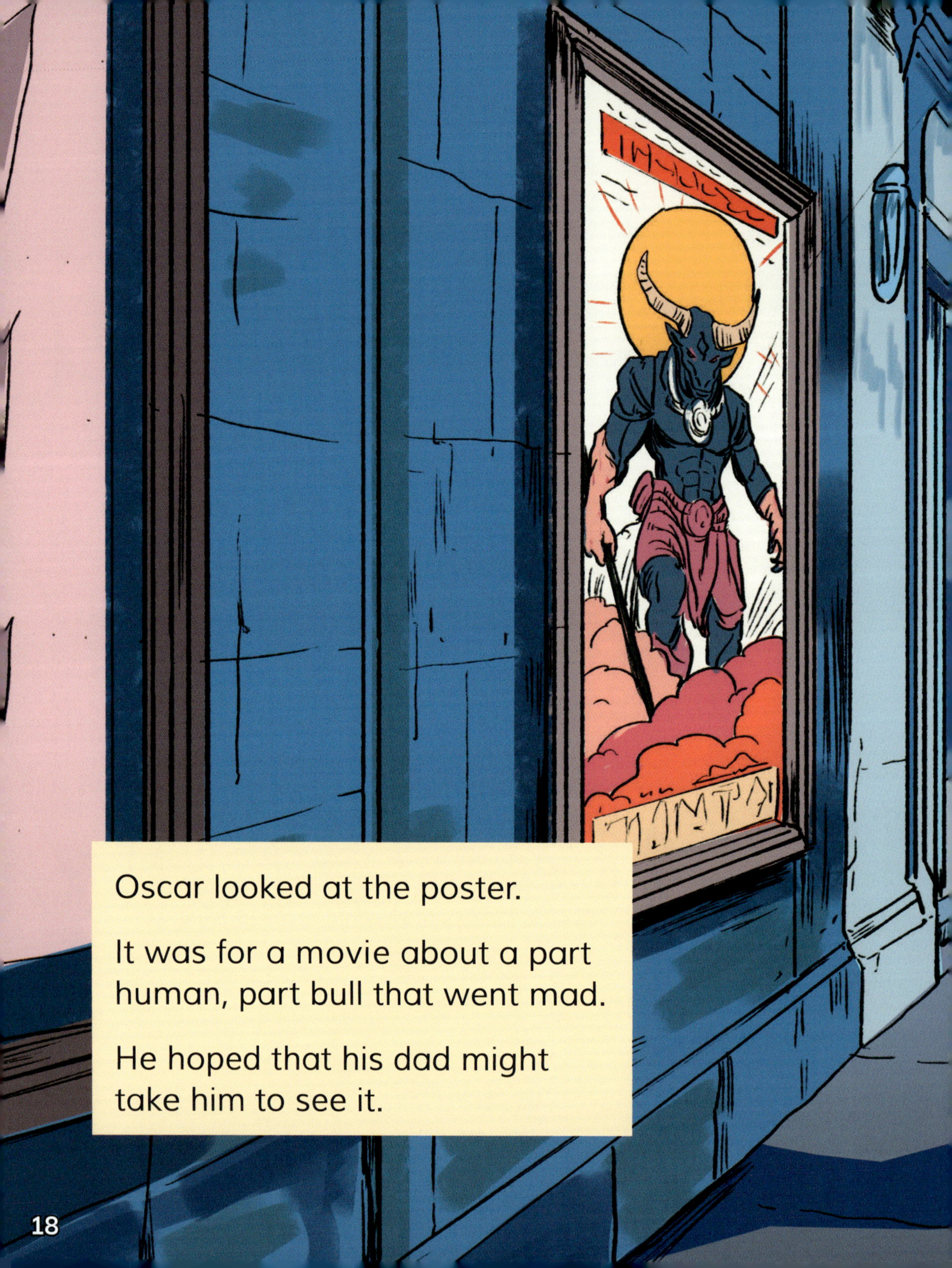

Oscar looked at the poster.

It was for a movie about a part human, part bull that went mad.

He hoped that his dad might take him to see it.

When Oscar got home, his father was back from work.

"Dad," called Oscar. "I want to see that new movie. Can we go and see it?"

"I'm afraid not," said Dad. "Too much work to do."

Oscar sighed.

If Dad didn't take him, he wasn't going to see the movie.

Oscar looked online to find something to do. With his mouse, he clicked on loads of sites.

Next Saturday, there was a big home game. He was up for that!

That afternoon, Oscar went to the stadium and got a pair of tickets. It was going to be a treat both for him and for Dad.

Oscar ran home with the tickets.

“Dad,” he called. “We’re going to the game on Saturday.”

“Oh no!” said Dad. “The bosses have piled so much work on me – I’ll have to pull out this time.”

Oscar put on a brave smile, but he was gutted.

The next week, Oscar was back online.

He spotted that DJ Mouse was playing soon. DJ Mouse was a cool rapper. Dad liked him too.

Oscar pushed the mouse around until the cursor rested on the ticket button.

"Dad," he called. "Will you pay for these tickets?"

Dad looked at the screen.

"Good plan, Oscar!" he exclaimed.
"I like DJ Mouse!"

Then he paused.

"Oh no!" he sighed.
"There is a work seminar that day. I cannot go."

"Work, work, work!" muttered Oscar.

"Let's do something next week," said Dad, feeling bad.

On the next Sunday, Dad found Oscar in his room.

“I have tickets for that new stand-up comic on Thursday night,” he said, putting the tickets on Oscar’s desk.

"My friend and I are going swimming that night," said Oscar.

"Oh," said Dad. "I did say I'd get tickets."

"You've been working so much, I just expected you to forget," said Oscar.

Dad sighed. "I haven't been a good dad, have I?"

"You are a good dad," said Oscar. "But sometimes you just forget what's important."

Oscar grinned as he grabbed his mouse. "Now, let's look for something next weekend that we can both do together."